Journal Entry

Jovan Mckoy

Cover art by Jovan Mckoy

Black Minds Publishing is a national publications platform centered around the personal and professional growth of artists and creatives of the Black diaspora. At Black Minds Publishing we aim to give more visibility to raw artistic works, both literary and visual, that center on the healing process of the Black mind, body and spirit. We aren't concerned with the rigid expectations of academia or the "supposed to's" of artistic gatekeepers and instead choose to prioritize genuine works that have meaningful impact for its readers.

Names: Mckoy, Jovan

Title: Journal Entry

Description: Philadelphia, PA: Black Minds Publishing [2020]

BLACK MINDS
PUBLISHING

Introduction

Growing up, I always had issues trying to express myself. I believed I had a voice that didn't matter, that my cries would just be a whisper to the masses. When I started writing poetry in high school, I finally started to hear myself, and I wanted others to hear my pain, my struggles and all the blessings that come with it. Poetry became therapeutic for me and gave me the chance to share my experiences.

This book is something I've been sitting on for years; this is me finally venting about my demons, my blessings, my love life, my blackness and whatever brings me joy with original artwork done by yours truly. This is a healing process. I'm glad to share with you all, my *Journal Entry*.

Acknowledgements

My Mom and Step-Dad - First and foremost, my parents have always had my back even when I didn't. When they found out I wanted spoken word to be my life and how passionate I was about it, they supported me full force with no questions asked. My parents were always present at my most important performances, and they rooted for me at the ones they couldn't attend. Through all of my decisions, good or bad, their hands were always there to catch me when I fell and to applaud me when I stood tall. I thank both of you for always believing in me and loving me with no hesitation. I love you both from the bottom of my spirit.

PYPM (Philly Youth Poetry Movement)- PYPM basically raised the poet in me. I honestly would be nowhere close to where I am today if it were not for this organization. Despite any ill feelings I may have had towards how things ended with them, I am more than grateful I was able to be a part of that family. I met most, if not all, of my closest friends through PYPM. Thank you Vision, Kavi, Greg and my many other mentors. I am beyond thankful for the opportunities and experiences that led to this book.

Breedlove/Fishbowl Family- When I turned 20 years old, I aged out of being a youth poet, but I was still seen as a youth artist whenever I performed. Christopher KP Brown gave me my first feature in the city, at an adult open mic called Pecola Breedlove and the Freedom Party. I felt more free and more of myself performing there. I ended up building a bond with the Breedlove staff: KP, Mizz Jasz, Enoch the Poet (who helped me with the making of this book), and other amazing poets who attended the event. I even became a host and eventually part of the family. Thank you for restoring my passion in spoken word.

JustMike - Mike brought me to a whole new audience and really challenged me performance-wise to feel comfortable no matter what crowd I perform for. He's introduced me to some of the most talented poets who, along with Mike, have given me many performing opportunities. Thank you for always giving me a chance and putting me "D" to the game.

Das Kader/The Crew - My closest friends, the squad, the gang. I met most of my close circle of friends through PYPM, so as you may guess, they are all writers. Some of the most talented rappers I know, they've always kept it real with me when it came to my art, whether I wanted to hear it or not. Through the years we don't see each other as often as we did in high school, but whenever we link, it's like we were with each other the day before. My homies always believed in me even through my trash poems; they kept reminding me how I was "that boul" when it came to poetry. I'm thankful for all of my brothers, and I hope I make them proud with this one.

My First Love - You've shown me so much about myself during our moments together. You were the first woman I could be transparent with both mentally and physically. When we were on bad terms, you always taught me something even when I was too stubborn to listen. You were always the first ear to hear my newest poems and the first pair of eyes on my new paintings. So much of you inspired my art. Thank you for loving me and my art unconditionally even when you didn't have to.

Table of Contents

Chapter 1: A "Me" Thing — 1

Bad News — 2

Wall Crawler — 6

Joker — 8

Parent's Normal Activity — 10

Bad News Pt. 2 — 11

Cherry — 14

David's Pantoum — 16

Shana's Sonnet — 17

Chapter 2: A "Black" Thing — 18

3 Days — 19

Bulletproof — 22

If They Lynch My Son — 25

Invite — 26

Real Niggas — 28

Chapter 3: A "Funny" Thing — 31

Black Men Don't Cheat Congregation — 32

Off The Clock — 36

Chapter 4: A "Love" Thing — 38

Avatar — 39

Limbo — 41

Herspective — 45

Distance — 46

Closed Doors — 47

Letter To My Future Wife   49

Type of Love (Inspired by Saul Williams)   52

Biography   55

Chapter 1: A "Me" Thing

Bad News

My house stinks of bad news.
The smell roams around the cracks
of rooms like rodents.

Why does depression always try to
make comfort in a home that doesn't
belong to it?

It makes me uneasy when I walk around
the house and see my mother with her 9-5
shift bags under her eyes.

Coming home from work with 5-9 bags in
her arms- groceries the size of continents-
she's always trying to carry the whole damn world on her shoulders.

I've wanted to ask her how her pregnancy felt.
Must be stressful carrying a burden for 9 months.
She avoids looking at my old baby pictures and bottles of booze.

I was seen more noose than newborn.
According to the stress marks marking
territory around her stomach,

I'm the reason her love life lacks love.
Her womb couldn't carry a baby and
butterflies simultaneously.

Fetus & flutter, those words can never
coexist. She says I'm not the reason her
butterflies went bitter, my birth father is.

He keeps her caterpillars in a jar.
Locked them in a closet-
never knew love could be claustrophobic.

Don't know how they fit between all them bones.
So deep, but oh so shallow.
Whenever I speak his name to her only

a hush follows. I understand why now,
a boy not knowing his biological
father keeps the Black boy's bio logical.

What isn't logical is abandoning fathers
are both blood and heavenly.
God has seemed to pass down the trait

of not supporting his children.
That's why I've never carried prayers in my pockets;
they weren't any help when bullets found refuge

in the ribs of my brother. My step dad sits on his bed,
melancholy, staring at the night sky
watching feathers from flocks of birds fall and

form a path that he follows, hoping it's my brother
coming to visit from heaven
lost on his way home.

He comes across death so much he sees
the reaper more neighbor than nuisance.
Parents hold so much shit in from rainy days

their guts turn into gutters; a mother shouldn't
have to lose any more flutter.
When my brother died I felt like my step dad

lost two sons that night.
I was blocked out, an eclipse.
I'm tired of holding so much shit in

tired, of carrying this constant self
conscious constipation constantly
seeing a dead carcass in my mirror

and vultures outside my window
hoping I don't carry on, so my body
can become carryon.

I'm tired of this stench of bad news.
I wonder, if I hold my breath long enough...

...will the smell go away?

Wall Crawler

I attach myself to people,
hold on to them like the energy
I give through my body is suppose
to be reciprocated at my whim.

I bare other's souls while struggling
to recognize my own. It's like a superpower,
like someone putting up a wall and me
clinging to it calling myself a savior,

knowing I'm just a self-saboteur,
slinging towards any direction that accepts
my embrace. I am my own toxic relationship,
my venom something symbiotic to my spirit.

The carnage it causes my mental health is a
burden super strength couldn't carry,
a threat to my own well being that I am scared to avenge.
Advice grows thin from any Aunt May or Uncle Ben.

It's like my conscience and my anxiety are the only
things I can vent to. These are the moments
that make me feel like Spider-Man, a wall crawler
looking for solid ground to balance on,

someone who only finds peace with Mary Jane,
whose only real high is when he's swinging from
heights trying to snatch the prayers God won't answer.
Am I an artist or an arachnid caught in its own webs?

My self conflict likes being both predator and prey.
My fingers numb, my eyes bloodshot nightly.
I smell nothing but dark liquor and backwoods;
I taste nothing. My senses are tingling and

telling me there's something detrimental
to my mental but all I see around is me.

Joker

I'm so happy that I don't know how to express my demons to people. A painted grin across my mouth is some of the most consistent art that I've done. I make a masterpiece from all of the pieces that don't fit. My friends believe my frowns are out of character, my parents believe me explaining how I feel is out of character, I can only be myself when I'm their entertainment. It's funny, everyone loves a clown until his wrists wound from juggling things far more heavier than he is. My room, Arkham Asylum. My city, Gotham. My God, doesn't understand my jokes like he used to. Even when I tell people I'm cracking the fuck up they fail to see the fractures in my voice.

Parent's Normal Activity

I've been haunted by a man who died
some years back. His spirit spares no trauma.
My mother speaks of him as if his body
was an omen, speaks his name as if it were
a curse, a tongue twister that makes every
sentence about him a natural disaster.

I see the post traumatic stress starting to possess her.
I don't know how this house became home for a hex
because I've prayed, danced, sung, but no hymn could
bring him back into existence. The living room walls
only know about this man by conversation.
His touch, a privilege we got used to not having.

His face, a Krueger comfortable in my nightmares.
He is a ghoul who tortured families he was once a part
of, a real life boogeyman that basks in the bed of the
skeletons in my closet. But out of all of the monikers
I give this monster, my mother still tells me not to call
him anything other than a ghost, especially not dad.

Because being raised by a ghost is a paranormal activity
which happens to be my parent's normal activity.
There's no exorcising this type of demon, no God
to pray to when your father gave you clouded judgement
of both the human and the heavenly.

Bad News Pt. 2

It's been a while since I sat down
on a church pew. Admitting my sins
at will is an act me and God ain't used to.

It's been a while since I've read psalms,
since I found peace in prayer. Now I just
pray in pieces and God don't believe in

the connection between my palms. Me and
my blessings have been coming to qualms
like me and my moms when my temper

gets too tempting. I still love her with every
inch of my soul. No need for a white picket fence or
mortgage over rent. She makes the most abandoned

houses still feel like home. She makes the most
abandoned people feel like home,
still she gets no credit for her effort or her gestures.

It don't make her body better; she be stressin,
I've been blind to the message, but still
everyday I look into mirrors,

tellin' myself today is the day for optimism.
My reflection never listens. I wish I was omnipresent,
more sufficient, so I can present to both of my parents

some new digs to release all the stress they be wearin'.
I still watch my momma's tears run more than sink faucets.
She can't even call on the calm in her own casa.

It's ironic how the landlord's God complex is colossus.
Drama the size of continents lay on her back;
the weight of the world fucking with her posture.

My father done fostered a fear of dying so dim
it fits in between the skeletons in the both of our closets.

11

I tell him to clean it and he says that he will.

He doesn't mean it, he's dealing with demons
and clashing with evil. I understand all of the
distance he has with people.

Being surrounded by so much death
Life starts to seem more lethal.

The devil's cocky.

God's too forgiving.

I been working these long shifts and friends
wonder why I'm moving different. High school
friends wonder why my music's different.

My writers block wonders why ain't my muse
been listening. The soles of my feet and the
feats of my soul have always had a limit.

You ever scream to God while everyone around
you reacts in silence? Sometimes I be so pissed
 it's hard for me not to react in violence.

Never asked for sympathy or a symphony
of small violins, just isolation on an island,
no S.O.S. It's kinda scary...

When I'm by myself I feel I'm at my best.
I hide it all behind the laughs I must confess,
I tried bibles for answers,

got spiritual with enchantments,
I wish I could halt adulting;
I took my childhood for granted.

Now I work a 9-5, check to check
to survive. For my moms
I promise I'll see 25.

Cross my fingers on my spine.
Black boy sorry for telling a white lie like,
Black boy will believe he can fly.

Momma I won't be no Icarus but the
intentions of my conscience is feeling
so mischievous.

Do better, I gotta get better
Life daily for me is spitting a persona,
been tormented by the demented.

Can't even find my Patronus,
no alakazam, presto, abracadabra,
hocus pocus can help me focus.

I'm the only person I should worry about
being hopeless. That's how I hold shit.
Anxiety daily has me feeling like moving

in the middle of the ocean,
and I can't swim.
Why drowning feel like culture?

For the past year it was hard for me to be
frank in poems. For the past year I wondered if I sank
will people still scream for the air in my lungs?

I'll save my last breath asking God what else I gotta give you?
It's been a while since I sat down on a church pew
Admitting my sins at will is an act that you and I ain't used to.

Cherry

Grown men brag
about popping cherries
But not about raising the seed

David's Pantoum

You dangle with the weight of death on your shoulders
but still you move like there's no eulogies on your spine.
The weight you're lifting doesn't get lighter, even when you get older.
I understand why you carry so heavy with due time.

Still you move like there's no eulogies on your spine,
raising a seed while trees around you wilt with the season,
I understand why you carry so heavy with due time.
You be a figure who fathers branches no matter the burden of his
demons,

raising a seed while trees around you wilt with the season.
I know you hold forests in your hands yet still pray between the splinters.
You be a figure who fathers branches no matter the burden of his
demons,
through the fruits of your labor I know sometimes the bites can get bitter.

I know you hold forests in your hands yet still pray between the splinters.
I know it's like stepping on twigs when you're lovesome;
through the fruits of your labor I know sometimes the bites can get bitter.

I just thank you and love you, for helping this black boy blossom.

Shana's Sonnet

You the best gift God could give a son
you my mother and you're my best friend
you the most beautiful miracle God has ever done
you the name I speak if my lungs lose wind

you a relief superhero, a woman of wonder
the first woman to show and teach me about loyalty
you both the calm before the storm and the crack of the thunder
the first woman to show and teach me my Black is royalty

ain't no one fight for me like you do, Ma Dukes,
only you wouldn't judge all of the skeletons I bear in my closet
ain't no one take flight for me when I jump sky high with no parachute
you're my heart, backbone and my conscience

Mother of mine, I got yo' back like neck got spine
and I'll always love you even when it's past our time.

Chapter 2: A "Black" Thing

3 Days

The first day that I
carried his body,
skin dark like the
night it was bathed
under, hollow, like a
shell that strayed too
far from its barrel,
I found him beaten.

          His palms chaliced and
          stiff like leather from a whip.
          The southern breeze brushing
          his rigamortis against the trees,
          they tell me that the smell is
          something familiar to them,
          the nooses hanging from their
          branches dangle like muscle

memory of his ancestor's
silhouettes. Their screams
still question the strange
fruit in my current.
They ask me who is this
boy? Where is his home?
Why folk like him always
hang around these neck of

          the woods? With his head
          laying against my waves
          like it's the only peace he
          has gotten in hours.
          He floats like a boat on
          calm water, his organs
          soaked in maggots.
          They rattle like chains

in his belly. The sound of
it gives my ripples deja vu.

Who could do this to a child?
To heist his freedom
and leave a barren vessel?
His face, a cool blue surface
like mine, we be related.
Did they think I could

      nurture his corpse? That I
      would adopt his death into
      my streams, raise this boy
      something like a lynching
      would? On the 2nd day I
      cradled his limbs under the
      sun. It danced around the
      barbed wire wrapped around

his throat, like God was
trying to loosen the grip.
Look at him, cotton gin
becoming part of his being.
His body, barely noticeable,
I wonder if any wandering
white eye just seen three fifths
of him above the water.

Look at him. I was given a
lifeless child, told to carry
him the way I did his ancestors,
in bondage, with my tides
like anchors, like something
Black, something burden heavy
on a ship. Carry him in water
like his mother, why are Black
women and I always seen as bearers of cemeteries?

They make them give birth to graves,
eulogies of innocents that make my water break

into a mausoleum for their offspring. A babysitter for their flesh, bones or
anything left of their spirit. On the third day, his screams still stretched

through all of Mississippi, reaching, like the way that woman claimed his arm reached around her waist, reaching, like a whistle may or may not reached towards her direction. Look at how his mother won't even recognize her baby. I know she must be somewhere clenching her Black womb like a white finger clinching the trigger on a gun. Look at him, his fingernails filled with blood and skin not kin to his, those men that gave a lifeless child to my river, they walk with the same wind in their lungs that they snatched from him. The gunpowder all intrusive in his wounds, dirt and ash oozing from his bones, his Black joy beaten into an invasion, his Blackness, never had a chance to defend itself.

Look at him….

                            Look at him….

                                                    Look at him….

Bulletproof

I ain't ever been a hero or
something to marvel at.

Just a man with mass incarceration
indicated in his surname.

I call myself Cage.
Free enough to have

never fought for a justice
that ain't ever fought for me.

And here you stand, dragging
your God complex and gunpowder.

I can feel the trembling beneath
your feet. The fear of your bullet slugs

ricocheting off my body as if this
is the first time you witnessed the durability

of a colored man. I wasn't born
bulletproof, that's a white man's privilege.

Didn't want to be the poster child for an
unwanted power. That's a burden even my

super strength could not carry
like fitting the description

playing "good negro" so
I could be a living one

my lifeless body being the
awkward silence in the room.

I'll always expect an officer to
Eric Garner the air from my lungs

at a stop and frisk. No matter how
extraordinary my strong may be,

a "nigga" must always be submissive,
a "nigga" must always remain calm during a lynching,
a "nigga" always has to be cool and collected under fire.

My natural rebellion sends shivers down your trigger finger,
leaving your berettas to find refuge in permeating our flesh.

Unleashing war on our skin until we're three-fifths of a body -
not whole enough to be human but enough of a fraction to fit in

your shackles. How dare you dangle a noose in front of me
and call it an amendment. You shuffle your badges through a graveyard

then blame the corpses for your destruction.
I'm just trying to be the captain this America never shielded.

Why does this country praise white men in armor
but arm their armies towards a man whose skin is his armor?

I wonder if Iron Man would get terrorized like this.
You were always lukewarm about the cage you forced

people to see me as. A prison clothed in dark skin until
you can benefit from me. They always need an avenger

until it's your own people who need the saving.
It's folk like you who turn this city into dust and

it's people to ash. You watch your guns dance
through Black bodies, drag our freedom into prisons,

give us the moniker of monkeys then shame us for our gorilla warfare.
How can you say that I am God-like, then crucify me where I stand?

You preach under the same church that you are burning.
I ain't ever want to be super negro, a guardian for the ghettos

or protector of the projects. Blood soaked sheets are the only
capes this hero has seen, the only costume you allow us to have.

I want our sons to idolize a man whose skin is a resistance.
I just fear that my invulnerability makes them believe that

we are all bulletproof.

If they Lynch My Son

If they lynch my son on the street
Don't tell me to respond with unclenched fists
and words pretty for Fox cameras.

Don't tell me the blood shed of my
baby was an unfortunate loss
when that shit was an assassination-

a 400 year hit on his ancestors.
His beautiful Black voice drowned in badges,
the burning of his body on the sidewalk

a bonfire for the boys in blue.
The media profiting from the footage of his embers,
don't tell me not to smash any screen that shows

his flame going out. Don't tell me violence
isn't the answer when it has ALWAYS been yours.
Don't tell me you don't see his skin as resisting arrest.

Don't tell me you won't use COVID-19 to mask his murder.
Don't hit me with that "all cops aren't bad" rhetoric.
When all the graveyards are bedding Black bodies.

Fuck the apologies!

Your white tears won't scrape their skin off of the cement,
won't bring back the Black joy that was. If they lynch my son,
I'll want blood, anarchy on their blocks as a protest.

I want them to burn.
I want their ashes,
for his...

invite

Welcome to the annual Black delegation cookout
a paradise with no rainbow but all color
where everybody and they grandma be
a gathering of nappy hair and good gossip
where the sun and water are the only things piercing our skin
like oxygen
like this is breathing
like this is proof of our consistency
there's no drowning here
we trade jokes like skin care products
stories, like prayer
it feels amazing to relate with someone that has the same wounds as you
carrying the same bones of our ancestors in their teeth
just enough space for the bones of
barbecue ribs to fit
enough room for the chicken thighs to ease in
the only dark meat that is singed here
sirens don't paint the block on this day
just a mosaic of sounds that show our children
enjoying an out of body experience
in a barren field with no bondage
shifting our bodies to the negro spirituals of the Migos
reciting Quavo's adlibs like hymns
screaming "mama!"
when I see her Mac & cheese
corners as dark as the men she loves
here, the most serious debates on Black culture have been spewed from
collard green covered lips
like yes, Martin was the best 90s sitcom
yes, Katt Williams be on some shit
nah,
ain't nobody make better sweet potato pie than the pain between my
mother's fingers
here we dance
til the sun sets to show it's blue face
dance
til the souls of our feet forget their spirit
play

Franky Beverly "Before I Let Go"
celebrate
in irony
celebrate
holding on to our genesis like our genocide is the next morning
here bodies swing on their own will
we electric slide to the sound of our own resilience with
a mix of Marvin Gaye
a calm blue sky is host to this jamboree of Black joy
this church of ham hocks brisket & buttermilk biscuits
this hollow ground,
for the children of those whose hollow bodies were hung above one.
Welcome to the cookout.

Real Niggas

I've met grown men who raise their gun
                         better than they do their children.
Who praise their peace
                         and not the one who saves.
Men, who bare arms full of comfort
                         and safe space for their daughters
but don't believe in the same thing
                         for someone else's.
Men who don't practice what they preach, who find God
                         in staring at women like objects,
like they can't object to the catcalls given out like sermons.
         It's ironic how the amens are caught inside the misogyny.

Question:
If men like you disrespect every woman legs you've come from,
how do you treat your mother?

Question:
How is it that you don't love these hoes and only the homies
but rock homophobia like those new Jordan's your child support paid
for?

I bet you spent so many moons repping your hood
                         that you don't even know what your own son looks like.
I don't understand you so called "real niggas"
                         Self proclaimed soldiers,
always finding war in the streets but ignoring
                         the ones going on in your own homes.

You "I got Gucci flip flops, but hardwood floors are all my child knows"
niggas.

You "I move that brick and wonder why I can't build a home" niggas.

You "Black lives matter...only if they from my hood" niggas.

Don't spit a sixteen about Trayvon
                         just to get your soundcloud poppin'.

Don't say your mixtape is fire and
              you ignore the flames burning around your community.
The ashes of Black bodies under your feet are just asphalt to you.

Don't brag about the Benz, Ferraris or Lambos
              that you can't afford.
We all know bandwagons are the only whip you
              real niggas seem to be pushing these days.
Most of our Black men have forgotten the value
              in their skin, the fight for each breath we take,
forgotten that we are kings,
              even when they have us down, Rodney
we will stand, Martin Luther
              march through these streets with something

stronger than these guns.
              March with our Black women,
our Black boys
              our Black girls.
I promise you the only thing I stay strapped with
              is my Black pride
because we are more than a target,
              we are the children of God's blessings
and the devil's failed attempts.
              We are the Kendrick Lamar's rapping on top

of police cars and the support for all the Beyoncé's
              willing to drown with one.

We are Black men.
We are beautiful.
We need to treat it as such.

Chapter 3: A "Funny" Thing

Black Men Don't Cheat Congregation

Public service announcement from the BMDCC
the Black Men Don't Cheat Congregation
the collective of faithful melanated brothas

First I'd like to say…

We do not claim every man who preaches to be kin to this church.
Don't claim men who're only faithful to what's convenient for their dick,
men who know pillow talk like the back of every woman who walks past,

the Harpos who have no answer when you ask, "who is this woman?"
who find God in every mattress but their own.
The BMDCC knows of no affairs but the ones of the Lord.

The Bible be the only Black book by our bedside
and no! Just because your man wears the "Black Men Don't Cheat"
t-shirt, does not mean that nigga ain't out here still cheating.

We don't claim the wolves in sheep's clothing.
We don't claim the ankh niggas,
the brothas who put the "ho" in hotep,

the ones who say namaste then leave when new ass reflects
off their crystals. The men who abuse their crown for the pussy,
who want to align your chakras for the pussy,

"What's ya zodiac sign?" for the pussy,
when they want to know how your moon rising,
know that's a double entendre for the pussy.

We know Kings be on some fuck shit too;
Coretta Scott knows better than anybody.
We don't claim the, "it's not what it looks like niggas."

Cause it's always what it looks like, nigga.
Looks like lying, looks like finding security
lying in between something different every night.

Black men love to say they're your rock
like Beyoncé ain't make lemonade for thirsty niggas like that
like Left Eye ain't finish the fire they sparked cause niggas like that,

like Madea didn't leave hot grits on the stove for niggas like that.
Black men be oblivious that sometimes they are the diary of a mad Black
woman, but Black men don't cheat.

Edit…

Some Black men don't cheat.
Don't bask in women like a boy in Baskin Robbins,
like the Black men that love their flavors.

Edit…

like the Black men that like most flavors.
We've watched fellas branch from women cut from the same tree as
them, Black men love you like you foreign.

They love that shit, they love everything that's isn't like they momma...
mocha...maybe only if she caramel. When you kiss him, now you know
why his lips taste differently each time...Black men be greedy.

They want their cake and side piece too.
Dessert after dessert, I don't think y'all understand;
they desert after dessert.

Black men love you alien,
like monogamy is extraterrestrial.
Black men love you more like men in Black,

neurolize the fuck nigga.
Black men love games like boys,
the club be their call of duty.

Black men don't cheat on Black ops but
will turn your relationship into modern
warfare with no hesitation

finding each casualty along the way sexy
because Black men love to brag about the bodies they've collected.
Damn sis those roses he got you sure match them flags.

You know he calls you a different moniker around the homies,
Black men code switch like Black folk during a job interview.
Lying like that habit happens to be second nature to you.

We know Tracy's baby daddy cousin's girlfriend Tisha seen you with the
jawn from 52nd and market two weeks ago, you ain't gotta lie Craig!
You ain't gots tah lieeeeee!!

If committing is too heavy of a burden,
why put the weight on someone else's shoulders?
Black men be better than that.

Black men need to love our women with the same energy we give our
mommas. Black men need to be loyal with the same energy we give our
niggas. Black men need to be honest with the same energy we give our

religions and maybe just maybe,
you will all have faith in the BMDCC,
the home of the prayer Ciara says on the side of her bed.
Maybe you will see that there are faithful Black men out here.

Off the Clock

The first time it happened...my anxiety didn't mind it no issue,
the weight of the pressure balanced on the edge of my back, bent to the
whim of any unjust law that spews from Caucasian lips. Posture as
crooked as the place that made it that way, my fingers started to shake
like my nerves don't know how to act around company. I couldn't
speak, my speech got lost in my teeth; hesitation was all I knew.

The first time... my manager asked me to stay a little later for my shift,
my heart sank into my ankles, in a matter of seconds my legs went from
bold to Bambi. He always asks this towards the end of the damn day!
Don't look at me crazy!! You know you do it! Lip locked for 7 hours,
I peeped the hidden vendetta in your work ethic.
Nigga you ain't slick!

Corporate core values always seem to be finessing, just like you are right
now! Don't try to point out that long ass line of customers.
Yes, I see them! I see the stress of rush hour dressed on my fellow
coworkers' faces. I understand the need for an extra hand to help,
but God told me to notice no evil and to only look forward to my
blessings.

And I'd stay honestly, but this company doesn't put enough weight in my
pockets to keep me grounded here. How can I aid you in saving a store
that self-sabotages? You ask of the impossible!
It's like asking me to be an anchor to an already sinking ship
that the customers wouldn't even mourn. While we're drowning, they'll
ask if our heads above water enough to get them a glass of some.

False: the customer is always right.
Fact: the customer don't be knowing shit because *I* work here.

These last few months had a brotha a "Nat Turner" kinda' livid,
irked from the bottom of the same soul that feels no place here.
My peace has no place here. I fake my smiles here so often
my loved ones at home have to deal with a bent grin.
Happiness as low as my income.

Man, this job got me so low that even my raises feel insignificant,

especially when I have to deal with the demons. Sorry, the "guests"
like the boujee "Post-Racism" white folk,
the ones who voted Obama for a second term,
the ones who aren't racist because they son's best friend be token.

Or, the Black folk who think you owe them something,
wearing their skin like a VIP access pass, nah fam.
You still gotta pay this $10.95 for your meal.
Don't get mad at me bro; I just work here!
Like how my district manager manages his ego,

it's above me now! Energy so low I have no choice but to leave it in
God's hands. My guy is good with the miracles and everyday
I pray for him to save me from this bondage.
Long days with no break shifting my body to break,
long nights preparing myself for next day's trauma.

My dreams always tucked under my uniform because it's not a part of
company standards. When it comes to their employees wellbeing, there
are no company standards. Their actions to provide a better work
environment are always stand still, neglectful enough to stress out my
optimism.

If I'm being honest, this job is the most toxic relationship I've ever been
in and being asked to stay is like asking me to love everything about
myself and bury it, so no, I can't stay; I'm off the clock. I don't care how
late I came in this morning, imma leave when the schedule says I'm
suppose to leave

with my aspirations and a free meal because...reparations,
and hopefully you'll see me tomorrow,

but if you don't....
that means I'm calling out sick.

Chapter 4: A "Love" Thing

Avatar

You used to see me as the last of my kind.
Men who could sweep you off of your feet
effortlessly, men who could bend the air
from your lungs, being the bridge between
your anxiety and spirit, your absence like
lightning on my back. The glow we had
dimming to Black, our flame wild like a
nation of fire. Our hearts sometimes at an
Agni-Kai, the way I feel around you like
my head is barely above water. Wind below
my chest motivates the butterflies that inhabit
there, like the times where I'm in a state and
you're the only one who can bring me back to
earth. I'm sorry I begged for you to keep me
grounded in the blind, that I begged for your
ocean tides when I couldn't even appreciate
the small ripples before them. I tried to save
your world without mastering the elements
within myself. I loved when you bore
my demons like it wasn't an act of my blood
bending, like I didn't have a savior complex,
like I don't live through my past lives,
like I don't disappear when war wages between us.

Limbo

When you're with him, does
the first syllable of my name
begin to slip from your lips?

Do they begin to shake like
the space between your fingers?
Like someone else's is trying to

make home in a foreign place
they don't belong. When you
hug him, does it feel like a foreign

place you don't belong to? Does
the surface of your skin get
nervous? Does it accept his touch

like it does mine? And when you
smile, does your grin welcome his
presence with the same amount of passion?

Like your heart sees him as equal
to everything peaceful about you?
When he speaks of his future daughter

does he use all of your facial features to
manifest her? My love, I miss your embrace
dancing through my bed frame.

My mattress still pillow talks about yours,
it knows you verbatim like muscle memory.
When you're alone do you reminisce about

the winters spent on it? Do your thoughts
still sleep on my springs? Will my hands
still be the haven for when you fall?

When you lay with me, do you still feel the
warmth of a summer? Or do we just have sex
and connection for a season?

Is the way that I try to love you seasoned?
I hope you didn't meet him with the same
cadence on your tongue. A sound I know

all too well. I pray your origin story with
him isn't a carbon copy of our panels.
I pray he hasn't been in your bed long

enough to see the monsters underneath it.
I wonder if it's me scratching at your floor
boards. I fear the four walls of your room

will slowly not be able to recognize my love
because Baby, I can feel it in my flesh and bones,
a feeling I know all too well.

To you I'm becoming nothing but a mere phantom
fantasizing about when we were both alive.
Now I'm just a zombie searching for any of your

organs to give me a reaction. Can you hear me
screaming your name from the same grave I dug
for myself? The mud sinking in my shoes.

Was this what it was like for you? Carrying around
dead weight? Calling it patience? Does he give you
patience? I know I don't know this man,

but I know he could never cater to your spirit like I do.
When you feel yourself nothing but a ghost I know he
doesn't make you feel human like I do.

I know he's just a mere muggle who doesn't understand
your witchcraft like I do. I know he can't handle your
Black magic, the voodoo and spells you put me under

are a feeling of bond or bondage; I'm not too sure
but it's a feeling I know all too well like our favorite
song playing and the lyrics in our message thread

becoming as thin as the ice we dance on. Does he
give you solid ground? A place to land when you fall?
Does the space next to him at night echo your name

more than I do? I think my sheets miss your palms
more than me. The walls of my shower still remember
your fingerprints. The steam on the porcelain tiles still

outline your silhouette. Does his home know your body
as well as he does? Does he know your favorite spots
behind and outside of closed doors?

Does he hate when you come over?
Is he prepared for what it feels like
to watch you leave?

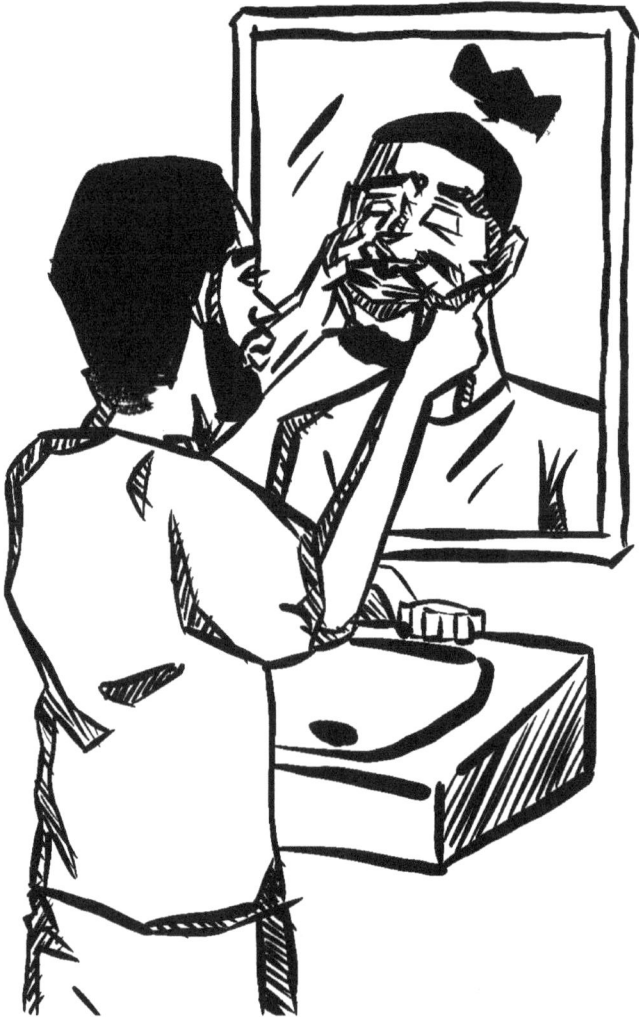

Herspective
From her eyes

I love this boy so much
I'm not sure if I have any left for myself.
He got a smile pretty enough for the both of us,
a summer spent finding warmth in his embrace
just to cry during the winters on his shoulder.
I love this boy so much
my body started changing seasons for him,
tried to please every part of him that couldn't
love me enough. His potential was what held
my feet to the floor.
Some nights we would cuddle
a fire between his palms and my thigh.
Some restless nights I'd watch him sleep in peace.
Look how I put his dreams before my own.
I love this boy so much
that I would clip my wings to craft feathers for his pillow,
be his Aphrodite and Icarus within the same breath.
This boy cares for me so well
my heart sees chivalry even in his demons,
sees the holes he punches in the wall as "breaking and rebuilding."
He covers them with his paintings,
it's just like him to hide his wounds behind something lovely.
I love this boy so much
I couldn't see the foreshadowing behind his canvas.
Ain't that his stress reliever?
Ain't that what I'm here for?
Isn't waiting my proof of loyalty?
Look how my patience is something creative,
just like him, a man with so many talents that
anything else close to him is just a hobby.
I love this boy so much,
even when I don't want to,
even when I shouldn't,
even when it doesn't feel mutual,
even when it doesn't feel...

Distance

girl you a whole snack
a full course meal
and then some
girl i miss you dancing
your lips calling me handsome
texting me from the bathtub
like your name rev run
love, you pump me up
you Joe Budden all my engines
why have you always been so far?
like there's not an "i" in distance
liking my pics on insta
don't mean you love the picture
girl do you love me sober?
or only when emotions mix in liquor
when i saw you i had to shoot my shot now we both triggered.

Closed Doors

i want your body in places our orgasms aren't familiar with yet
i want every room to feel you like my palms do
i want to find vacation on every part of you that's vacant
your body an island and i've never been so sure to
swim to your shore
you ride like midnight ocean tides
i love you wet like atlantic
deep under your water, baby i give you my lungs
my fingers dancing in your waves
i rub them on my lips
you taste just like sugar and margaritas
something like honey and candy
everything sweet on my tongue
your moans music to my ears
a choir humming under your dress
you sound like every room we're in has thin walls
i want them to whisper about all the nasty sung between our privates
i want you loud enough to wake up the public
i want full disclosure on all the parts of you that you allow me to cater to
because i love when you visit my bedroom,
you always cum with that beautiful smile.

Letter to My Future Wife

Dear Queen,
babe,
boo
or any other alias that validates us,

my first love,
rib,
oxygen,
anything that makes me feel more human,

my sugar,
honey,
sweet thang
know how good you taste when I speak your name.

Know how home my house feels everytime you walk
through the door. When I propose I promise to be on
both knees, ring in between my palms,
scripture on my lips,

asking you to love me for a lifetime like a sinner
begging God to answer his prayer.
We make anywhere our church
even if the pews around were empty.

You and God will be all the congregation I
need to wed that soul. It's the least I could do for you.
Our vows aren't all I owe you for all the times
you loved me like it was an obligation.

When you see your parent's relationship in our arguments,
when the honeymoon starts to turn into sour mornings
and the grip in between our fingers starts to loosen like truth with liquor,
I promise to still be the man I was the night before,

to still be your safe space when everything seems to be out of orbit,
to not bring you down to earth but to bring that shit to your feet.
I want to hear ever part of your day, the good, the bad

and ain't no ugly in your 24 hours. I want you to be all
up in my face 24/7. Remember every detail of my grin,
hold on to it in the moments you can't stand to be in my presence.

I want you past, future and present,
I want you both gift, giver and present,
I want you crazy for me after all the madness I present.
I promise nothing but love to you through sickness and health

until our bones grow brittle, death won't even do us apart.
I know you and I will still be turning up in the afterlife,
you smiling while throwing it back is the only pearly
gates I care to see.

I know heaven wouldn't be able to handle us.
Even when we can't handle us,
I promise to try.

Love,
 Someone who'll meet you half of the way

type of Love (inspired by Saul Williams)

Girl you got that type of love that
make a man want to write a love poem for you EVERY morning,
type of love where you love them jawns even if they're corny,
type of love like Bonnie and Clyde
or better yet Donna and Eric Forman.
You got that love that make real love feel so foreign,
love like when I'm in a Gump
you make me feel like Forrest,
type of love where you show me you're a different girl,
that 90s love, that Whitely to my Dwayne Wayne.
You show me a different world type of love,
fight for you like Martin type of love,
that for you I'd enter any arena,
That DAMN GINNNNAAAA type of love,
love where everytime I see you I bite my bottom lip,
that no matter how much your size change I'll always love how those
jeans fit type of love.
That you pose, I paint, type of love,
that dance in the rain, do it for Lil Saint type of love,
that whatever you serve me I'll clean my plate type of love.
Even without the charm,
your type of love makes me feel like I'm the luckiest man.
I find church in your arms and see an angel when
you give me your wingspan,
the type of love that'll have God be my wingman.
He be like, "on my Bible she be a bad jawn,"
the type of woman you have no choice but to pray for,
the type of love where you make me feel like Superman,
fuck is the cape for?
You're my Lois Lane during my lowest lane,
my restart button and extra life in any game,
type of love where I'll promise you home even if I only carry a brick,
type of love where you call me on ya break to complain about work, even
if you only an hour into ya shift,
type of love where I'd always fall for you but I'd never trip.
Girl you got that "Ex who??" type of love, that
"Text who??" type of love,
that "you the only one my spirit wants to be next to" type of love,

52

that "great sex" type of love,
that "I ain't talking about my clothes when I ask you to throw it back"
type of love, that how we supposed to make music without any strings
attached type of love,
type of love that'll battle the monsters in the back of my conscience.
If I'm honest I love the wars you fight everyday,
I love that formation you do, I applaud it.
Like a Bey fan at a Beyoncé concert,
that type of love that even when we married I'll still be the thirstiest guy
under ya comments,
type of love where I love to see you naked
and I'm talking about what's under your undergarments,
type of love where I call you "baby" even when I'm livid,
even when our views are different,
type of love where you're my rib, lung, heart and
anything else that keeps me living.
That love where I got ya' back even if my spine went missing,
that type of love where our dates are so long that time isn't in our vision,
type of love where it makes me want to give you and your anxiety the
same kind of attention,
that with you I would find religion even if my God went missing.
You my holy preservation, I can't be Hindu or Buddha,
type of love where I can't be peaceful unless you're part of the
meditation. So blunt you're part of the medication,
type of love where you're my partner, priest and my education,
love like if I lost my memories today,
tomorrow I would fall for you with no hesitation,
type of love where you love the little things like
"How was work?"
"Did you eat?"
"When you come home me and the bed are waiting"
Netflix debating,
Leading to naked bathing,
type of love that laughs at my jokes even when they cheesy,
that we go together like cheese and nachos,
like Wanda and Cosmo, you make my mind wander the cosmos.
In a few years I see you and I making love in our household,
a strong foundation that's how a house holds type of love.
No lie, it's true, and I love that I'll always have a type of love poem,
just for you.

Biography

Jovan Mckoy is a spoken word poet and visual artist from Southwest Philadelphia. His work is a fusion of Black liberation and the nuances of humor and joy involved in its pursuit. As a youth, he performed and honed his poetic skillset as a member of the Philly Youth Poetry Movement, affectionately known as PYPM. Earning a spot on their national youth team, Jovan has performed in multiple cities across America. In 2015, his team competed in the Brave New Voices international spoken word competition and brought home a championship for the city of Philadelphia. Post PYPM, Jovan served as co-host for a popular Philly open mic event, Pecola Breedlove and the Freedom Party. Off-stage Jovan is a multifaceted artist learning the best ways to blend his many talents. He believes making a living is doing what you love, and loving what you do; there's no exception.

www.ingramcontent.com/pod-product-compliance
Lightning Source LLC
Chambersburg PA
CBHW081141090426
42736CB00018B/3439